THE
PASTA
BOOK

Pinelli f 1835 Roma

THE

PASTA

BOOK

Recipes in the Italian Tradition

Julia della Croce

Illustrated by Laura Cornell

CHRONICLE BOOKS

SAN FRANCISCO

Library of Congress Cataloging-in-Publication Data available.

ISBN 0-8118-1745-8

Historical illustrations on pages 8, 13, 22, 25, 49, 57, 59, 71 courtesy of Museo Storico degli Spaghetti, Collezione Agnesi, Pontedassio (Imperia), Italy. Historical illustration on page ii from Raccolta di Costumi Romani, courtesy of the Spencer Collection, The New York Public Library.

Cover illustration by Kathy Warinner.
Cover design by Aufuldish & Warinner.
Book design by Brenda Rae Eno.
Composition by Wilsted & Taylor.

Printed in Hong Kong

Distributed in Canada by Raincoast Books
8680 Cambie Street
Vancouver, British Columbia V6P 6M9

10 9 8 7 6 5 4 3

Chronicle Books
85 Second Street
San Francisco, California 94105

Web Site: www.chronbooks.com

For my darling little girls, Gabriella and Celina,
the insatiable pasta eaters,
whose lives on this planet began with stelline.

TABLE OF CONTENTS

A Mythical Food,
a Misunderstood Food

Italian folklore is full of references to the magical properties of *i mac-cheroni*—dried pasta. It has been called everything from an aphrodisiac to a sedative. It has even been maligned as an opiate. Whatever skeptics might say, current scientific literature supports the folk belief that pasta helps people feel happy and calm. The complex carbohydrates in durum wheat, from which macaroni products (what the Italians call *pasta secca*) are made, stimulate the release of a chemical in the brain called serotonin, which has a calming effect on the human nervous system.

It is hard to imagine that when the first wave of Italian immigrants introduced their beloved pasta to these shores, it was considered unwholesome, strange, and even unsavory by most Americans. Today, it is wildly popular. But with the enthusiasm has come little understanding of how to cook it to its best advantage, a great deal of confusion about the differences between dried and fresh pasta, and the best ways to cook and sauce each variety.

The most simple, nourishing, inexpensive, and accessible form—the hard, factory-produced variety made with semolina (flour made from durum wheat) and water—is ironically the most misunderstood. The widespread notion persists in this country that dried pasta is inferior to fresh, homemade pasta, or what is passed off as "fresh" pasta by the booming specialty foods industry. Contrary to popular belief, hard, factory-made pasta made with semolina (a complex carbohydrate) water is more healthful than fresh pasta made with refined white flour (a simple carbohydrate) and eggs, and contains no fat or cholesterol. In the Italian kitchen, *pasta secca* is not considered inferior to homemade pasta. It is simply treated differently, because its more robust flavor and firm texture make necessary different cooking and saucing considerations.

What is sold as "fresh pasta" at a premium price in gourmet shops and, now, supermarkets has neither the health advantages of *pasta secca*, nor the flavor advantages of true handmade egg pasta of the kind that is still prepared fresh daily in many Italian homes. This commercial variety of so-called fresh pasta is rubbery and flavorless. Real homemade pasta is incredibly thin, delicate, and tasty.

Because the attributes of dried pasta so suit our health-conscious and time-short modern lives, this nutritious super-food is the focus of this little book. Along with recipes, I set forth guidelines for cooking and saucing it to its best advantage.

Matching Dried Pasta
Shapes to Pasta Sauces

The many shapes of dried pasta make it a fun and versatile food, but a little bit of sauce savvy will make it all the more enjoyable. Despite such whimsical names as *tirabaci* ("kiss catchers"), *ave marie* (prayers), *amorini* ("little loves"), and linguine ("little tongues"), every one of these little semolina-and-water sculptures has a purpose.

Various types of pasta work best and *taste* best when combined with certain sauces. Different shapes, due to their characteristic size and thickness, absorb and combine with sauces in different ways. And the density of dried pasta affects its flavor to a startling degree. For example, the flavor of *capelli d'angelo* ("angel's hair") is very different from that of rigatoni (large grooved macaroni), sauce not considered.

In general, the flavor and texture of dried pasta make it suited to robust and rustic sauces. (Other principles apply for saucing true fresh pasta.) In the authentic Italian kitchen, dried pasta is combined with sauces made from ingredients and flavorings that are characteristic of peasant cuisine—olive oil or salt pork, tomatoes, combinations of vegetables, beans, olives, fish, and economy cuts of meat.

Tomato sauces and simple "sauces" of butter and cheese combine easily with almost any type of pasta, dried or fresh, except for the smallest pasta shapes designed for soups.

Grated cheese, either parmigiano-reggiano or *pecorino*, is sprinkled on many Italian pasta dishes. But it is a mistake to assume, as many Americans

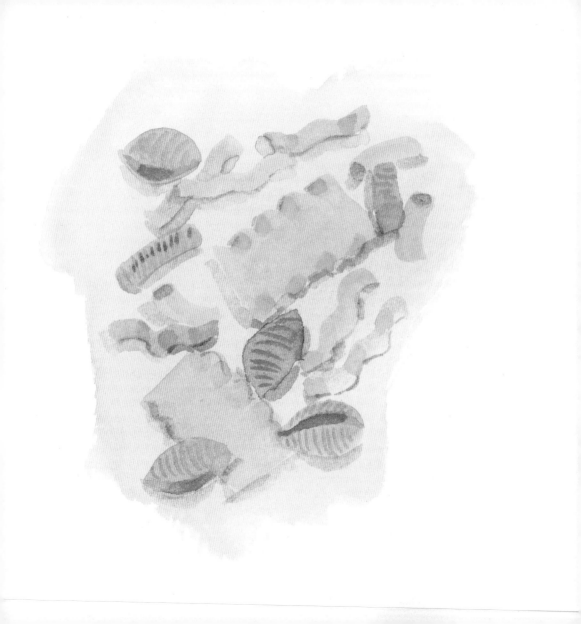

do, that it should indiscriminately accompany *all* pasta dishes. The flavors of these cheeses are simply not compatible with everything. They should never, for example, be sprinkled on seafood sauces.

Here are some further guidelines:

String or Ribbon Pasta　From the thinnest *capellini* to thick *bucatini*, long dried pasta shapes combine best with oil-based sauces. The oil easily covers each strand from end to end, keeping it well lubricated without oversaucing. These pasta shapes don't combine well with most meat sauces, except those in which the meat has disintegrated into small pieces. Large chunks of meat fall to the bottom of the plate instead of being evenly distributed through the pasta strands. Delicate sauces, such as those made with chicken livers, or seafood sauces are fine with these pastas. Vegetable sauces in which the ingredients are sliced very thin are suitable for all but soup-type "angel's hair," which should be used only in broths (see *Soup Pasta* below). The slightly thicker *capellini* are suitable with very fine, sieved sauces, or brothy seafood sauces.

Macaroni　Short, stubby varieties, such as elbows and *pennette* ("small quills"), and such shapes as *farfalle* ("butterflies"), *fusilli* ("corkscrews"), and *radiatori* ("radiators") are easily covered by thick cream or cheese sauces. The large tubular types, such as *ziti* ("bridegrooms") and *penne* ("quills"), are perfect for capturing meat and beans and such, which nestle in all the little tunnels and grooves. The largest shapes, such as *lumaconi* ("giant shells") and cannelloni ("very large reeds"), are designed to be stuffed.

Soup Pasta   Fine *capelli d'angelo* ("angel's hair") shaped into nests, and light, tiny *stelline* ("little stars") are designed for broths. The smallest shapes, called *pastine* (plural of *pastina*), combined with butter and milk, are typical baby food in Italy. Slightly thicker shapes, such as *acini di pepe* ("little pepper pods") and *semi di melone* ("melon seeds"), can be used in broths and light soups. *Tubettini* ("little tubes") and *conchigliette* ("little shells") work well in such robust soups as lentil and vegetable. In hearty minestrone that contains large beans and pieces of meat, the larger *ditali* ("thimbles") and *lumachine* ("small snails") work well.

The Golden Rules of Perfect Pasta

Always use the best pasta available, such as an imported Italian pasta. Look for all the attributes of a superior-quality pasta. It has a golden color, with a vaguely transparent quality; it is not pale and opaque. It has a clear, nutty perfume, and an equally clear, wheaty flavor. It retains its resistance to the bite, and its elasticity, even after cooking (as long as it's not overcooked). Last, look for the absence of excessive cloudiness in the cooking water after the pasta has cooked.

Always cook pasta in plenty of boiling water (4 to 5 quarts per pound of pasta, increasing the amount of water proportionately for larger quantities of pasta). Stir the pasta as soon as it is dropped into the boiling water, and keep stirring with a long-handled fork to prevent the pasta from sticking together. Never add oil to the pasta pot—it will coat the pasta and cause it to repel the sauce instead of absorb it.

Always salt the cooking water (unless salt must be eliminated for health reasons). Pasta cooked in unsalted water is virtually tasteless.

Never overcook pasta. Cook dried pasta al dente, "to the tooth." The cooking time will depend on the shape and thickness of the pasta. (Fresh pasta can never be cooked al dente because it is soft to begin with.) Follow the package directions for cooking time, and taste-test to judge for yourself. If in doubt, remove the pot from the burner—the pasta will continue to cook in its own heat for several minutes. Many Italian cooks add a glass of cold water to the pot as soon as the burner is turned off to arrest the cooking process. Then drain the pasta. It is important to use a colander that drains the water as quickly as possible in order to prevent the pasta from overcooking as it drains.

Don't overdrain pasta. Pasta should still be somewhat moist when combined with sauce. Otherwise, the pasta becomes too dry. Pasta should be well drained only when combined with very brothy, thin sauces, such as clam sauce, or an uncooked tomato sauce that contains abundant natural juices. Some sauces, such as unctuous pesto or thick cheese sauces, require a good deal of the pasta cooking water to thin the sauce out and keep the pasta moist.

Never rinse pasta after draining unless preparing it for a dish that will be further cooked in the oven, such as *apasticcio* or lasagne. In these dishes the noodles are deliberately undercooked, allowed to cool, layered in a casserole with other ingredients, and cooked in the oven.

In the true Italian style, serve pasta piping hot. In the authentic Italian kitchen, pasta is never served lukewarm or cold.

Whenever possible, use ingredients that are authentic in order to achieve the true flavors of Italian cooking.

Use the best-quality, freshest ingredients you can find. They will affect completely the flavor and the aesthetics of what you cook.

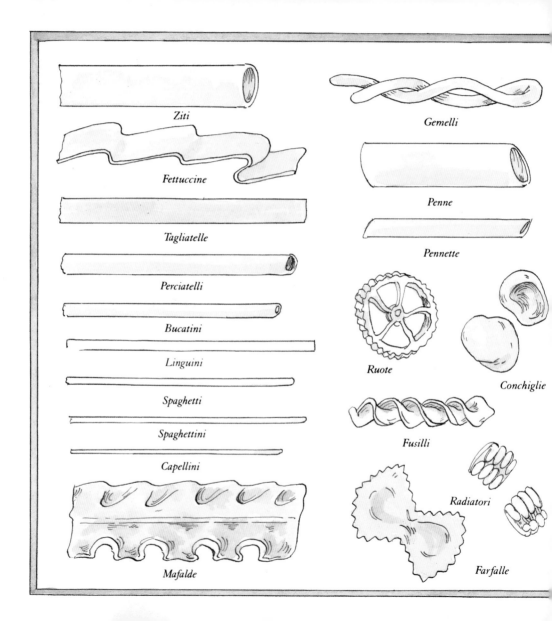

Ziti

Gemelli

Fettuccine

Penne

Tagliatelle

Pennette

Perciatelli

Bucatini

Linguini

Ruote

Spaghetti

Conchiglie

Spaghettini

Capellini

Fusilli

Radiatori

Mafalde

Farfalle

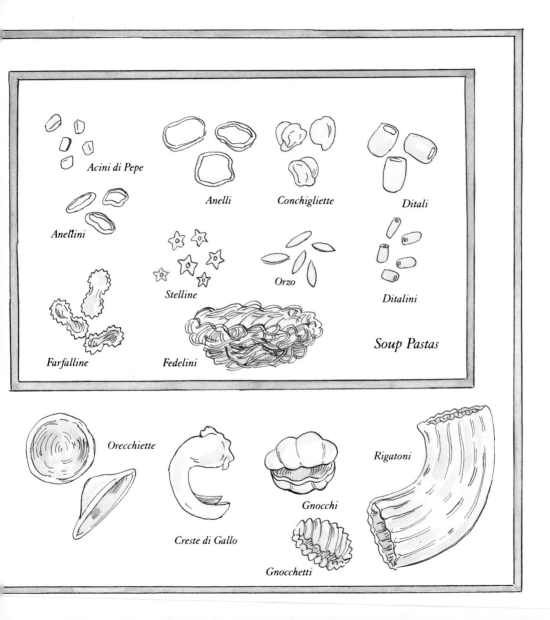

Acini di Pepe

Anelli

Conchigliette

Ditali

Anellini

Stelline

Orzo

Ditalini

Soup Pastas

Farfalline

Fedelini

Orecchiette

Creste di Gallo

Gnocchi

Rigatoni

Gnocchetti

Capelli d'angelo in brodo
"Angel's Hair" in Broth
for 6 people

"Angel's hair" has become very fashionable in America. Unfortunately, it is most often combined with all manner of sauces that are simply not compatible with it. Because the pasta is so fine, sauces do not flow easily between the strands, but rather fall to the sides and gather at the bottom of the plate. *Capelli d'angelo,* as the Italians call this form of pasta, is designed to be cooked in broth, or combined with only the most delicate, sieved, light, smooth sauces. The broth—Italian chicken soup—is never crowded with vegetables, meat, or pasta. It is simply clear and flavorful, made with vegetables and boiling fowl—the tastiest of birds for soup. The broth is strained after cooking and only a handful of some type of soup pasta added. Grated parmigiano is served at the table. The chicken is eaten as a second course with a piquant green sauce (*salsa verde*) made with olive oil, parsley, capers, and anchovies. Because boiling fowl is hard to come by in American markets, I have substituted chicken. However, if using boiling fowl, add more water until the bird is covered, and double the cooking time.

....

4 pounds economy chicken parts,
   such as backs, necks, and wings,
   or 1 chicken (4 pounds), cut up
1 medium yellow onion, unpeeled
1 medium carrot, scraped and
   halved
1 large stalk celery, including leaves

1 bay leaf
3 sprigs fresh Italian parsley and
   stems from a small bunch of
   parsley
enough cold water to cover (about
   12 cups)
1 fresh or canned tomato, cut up

¹/₄ teaspoon whole black or white
   peppercorns
1 tablespoon salt, or to taste
6 ounces capelli d'angelo ("angel's
   hair"), broken up, or "angel's
   hair" in nests, or soup pasta such
   as semi di melone ("melon
   seeds") or orzo ("barley")
freshly grated parmigiano, for the
   table

Wash chicken well in cold water, inside and out. Put all ingredients except pasta and cheese in an 8-quart stockpot. Partially cover pot, bring water to a boil, then gently simmer for 1 hour, skimming continually to remove scum. Strain stock and return it to pot. Use chicken for second course or reserve for some other use; discard all vegetables, herbs, and spices. Taste stock and add salt if necessary, bring to a boil, and add pasta. Stir, then cook over medium heat until pasta is tender but not mushy, 4 to 5 minutes. Serve immediately, passing grated cheese at the table for the soup.

Variation: Substitute 4 pounds beef shin, shank, or short ribs for chicken to make beef broth. Or combine beef and chicken for a mixed broth.

Conchiglioni ripieni di ricotta, mascarpone, e spinaci
"Big Shells" Stuffed with Ricotta, Mascarpone, and Spinach
for 4 or 5 people

Here is a light version of a classic treatment for stuffing dried pasta in the form of giant shells, nests, or *manicotti*. The sauce is cooked *al crudo,* that is, all the raw ingredients are cooked at once rather than the tomatoes being added to a *soffritto* of oil or butter, onion or garlic, and so on. This simple method of cooking produces a sauce with a fresh, clear tomato flavor. The mixture of stewed tomatoes, carrot, and onion is then passed through a strainer to obtain a smooth sauce. Virgin olive oil is added at the last. The lovely fruity oil both enhances the flavor of the sauce and leaves its own clear flavor. When in season, Swiss chard can be substituted for spinach.

~~~~~

Sauce
*1 can (28 ounces) plum tomatoes in
their own juice*
1 small carrot
½ small onion
*3 or 4 large fresh basil leaves (if un-
available, omit)*
2 tablespoons virgin olive oil

Filling
1¼ pounds (2½ cups) ricotta cheese
1¼ pounds fresh spinach

*scant ¼ teaspoon salt, for cooking
spinach*
1 egg, lightly beaten
½ cup freshly grated parmigiano
*scant ⅛ teaspoon nutmeg, prefera-
bly freshly grated*
¼ teaspoon salt
freshly milled black pepper to taste

*1½ tablespoons salt, for cooking
pasta*

8 ounces conchiglioni *("big shells")*
    or giant nidi *("nests")*
2 to 4 tablespoons freshly grated
    parmigiano, for sprinkling over
    pasta

To make the sauce, combine tomatoes and half their juice, carrot, onion, and basil in a saucepan. Bring to a boil and immediately reduce to a simmer. Cook over medium-low heat for 45 minutes with the cover partially askew, stirring occasionally. Tomatoes should simmer gently, or they will overcook and lose their clear flavor. Let mixture cool somewhat, then pass it through a food mill or strainer, which will remove all seeds and make a perfect purée of all the vegetables. (A food processor is not a substitute for a food mill, because it will not remove seeds and fibrous parts of vegetables.) Season purée with oil and set aside. Meanwhile, to make the filling, place ricotta in a sieve to drain off excess moisture, about 30 minutes. Thoroughly wash spinach to remove any sand, then discard any yellow or discolored leaves and all stems. Steam spinach, or cook in boiling salted water to cover, until tender but not overcooked. If boiled, drain well, re-

serving water the spinach has cooked over, then squeeze as much water as you can from spinach. Chop spinach finely; it is best to do this by hand. If you are using a food processor, be careful not to turn spinach to mush. Meanwhile, to cook the pasta, add enough cold water to reserved spinach water to make 6 quarts and bring to a rapid boil. Add the 1½ tablespoons salt and pasta and cook for 15 minutes. Drain. Refresh pasta with cold water to prevent it from sticking together. Set aside. To finish filling, beat egg with drained ricotta until smooth, then mix in spinach and remaining filling ingredients. Preheat the oven to 375°. Smear the bottom of a 10- by 14-inch baking pan with 2 to 3 tablespoons of the sauce. Using a teaspoon, stuff pasta shells with filling. They should be generously full but not so stuffed that they are wide open. Place stuffed pasta in pan and drizzle sauce over all. Sprinkle with parmigiano, cover with foil, and bake until sauce is bubbly, 20 to 30 minutes. Serve immediately.

The Atlantic Macaroni Co.

MILLERS AND MANUFACTURERS OF MACARONI FANCY PASTE & EGG NOODLES

THE ATLANTIC MACARONI CO.

MACARONI PLANT CAPACITY 100,000 LBS DAILY OF ALIMENTARY PASTE

295-303 VERNON AVE.
LONG ISLAND CITY
NEW YORK

Farfalle con peperoni rossi e gialli

"Butterflies" with Roasted Red and Yellow Peppers

for 4–6 people

The sauce in this dish is compatible with almost any string or ribbon type of pasta except "angel's hair." Most macaroni type of pastas are also suitable except for small *pastine* or large tubular shapes.

....

2 medium yellow bell peppers
2 medium red bell peppers
½ cup extra virgin olive oil
1 large clove garlic, chopped
salt and freshly milled black pepper
   to taste
1½ tablespoons salt, for cooking
   pasta
1 pound farfalle

Roast peppers on an open grill or in the oven until they are charred all over and tender inside. When cool enough to handle, remove skin, cut in half, and scoop out seeds. Chop fine with a knife or *mezzaluna* ("half moon") chopper. Do not use a food processor, which will purée rather than chop, causing the brilliant red and yellow of the peppers to blend rather than retain their separate colors. Combine with oil, garlic, and salt and freshly milled pepper to taste, and set aside. To cook the pasta, bring 4 to 5 quarts water to a boil and add the 1½ tablespoons salt and pasta. Stir, continuing to stir frequently to prevent pasta from sticking together. Taste pasta after 7 minutes; it should be cooked thoroughly but still be firm to the bite (al dente). If necessary, continue cooking. If in doubt, drain immediately—pasta will continue to cook while it is hot. Take care not to overdrain; pasta should be piping hot and still dripping a little when it is transferred to a serving bowl. Combine hot pasta with sauce. Serve immediately.

Note: This sauce can be made and refrigerated several days in advance of use. Use it cold or at room temperature, but don't heat it.

Farfalle con ricotta e spinaci

"Butterflies" with Ricotta and Spinach

for 3 or 4 people

Cheese sauces need a substantial but short pasta to carry them. The spinach in the sauce of this dish is trapped in the pleats of the *farfalle* ("butterflies"). Likewise, it would be caught in between the spirals of such shapes as *fusilli* ("twists") and *gemelli* ("twins"), or become trapped in the hollows of *creste di gallo* ("cockscombs").

......

¼ pound fresh spinach, thoroughly washed

1 teaspoon salt, for boiling spinach

8 ounces (1 cup) ricotta

1 egg yolk

¼ cup freshly grated parmigiano, plus more for the table

¼ teaspoon nutmeg, preferably freshly grated

¼ teaspoon salt

freshly milled black pepper to taste

1½ tablespoons salt, for cooking pasta

12 ounces farfalle, fusilli, gemelli, *or* creste di gallo

2 tablespoons sweet (unsalted) butter

Wash spinach thoroughly to remove sand, then discard any old or discolored leaves. Steam spinach, or boil in salted water, then drain and squeeze dry. Cool and chop fine. Mix 2 teaspoons tepid water with ricotta. Add egg yolk, the ¼ cup parmigiano, nutmeg, the ¼ teaspoon salt, and pepper. Stir mixture until creamy, then mix in cooled chopped spinach. Meanwhile, bring 4 quarts water to a rolling boil. Add the 1½ tablespoons salt and pasta and stir, continuing to stir until pasta is cooked al dente. Drain, being careful not to overdrain; pasta should still be almost dripping. Combine pasta with butter and ricotta sauce. Reserve some of the water in which pasta has cooked in case you have overdrained pasta (moisture from cooked pasta makes sauce smooth and creamy). Serve immediately. Pass parmigiano at the table.

Fusilli con zucchini alla Camilla

Camilla "Corkscrews" with Creamy Zucchini Sauce

for 4–6 people

Here is a recipe given to me by Camilla Destefanis for a very quick, delicious pasta dish in the summer, when zucchini are at their prime. In fact, once the zucchini are cooked, the sauce is practically instant. Select young, tender squash for the sweetest, tastiest sauce.

......

1½ pounds young zucchini, diced
2 tablespoons salt, for cooking
  zucchini
3 tablespoons sweet (unsalted) butter
1 cup (8 ounces) mascarpone
½ cup freshly grated parmigiano,
  plus more for the table
⅛ teaspoon freshly grated nutmeg
salt and freshly milled black pepper
  to taste
1 pound fusilli *("twists"),* penne
  ("quills"), or gemelli *("twins")*

Add zucchini and 2 tablespoons salt to 4 to 5 quarts rapidly boiling water and cook until zucchini are tender. Lift it out with a slotted spoon (reserving the cooking water) and transfer to a colander, then press on zucchini with a wooden spoon to expel excess water. Finely chop cooked zucchini by hand or in a food processor, or mash with a fork. If using a food processor, be careful—zucchini should retain some of its texture, not become puréed. Add butter, mascarpone, the ½ cup parmigiano, nutmeg, and salt and pepper to taste. Set sauce aside. Return zucchini cooking water to a boil and add pasta; stir and continue to stir frequently to prevent pasta from sticking together. Taste pasta after 9 or 10 minutes; it should be cooked thoroughly but still be firm to the bite (al dente).

If necessary, continue cooking. If in doubt, drain immediately—pasta will continue to cook while it is hot. Take care not to over-drain; pasta should be piping hot and still dripping a little when it is transferred to a serving bowl. Transfer pasta to bowl, pour sauce over top, and toss. Serve immediately. Pass parmigiano at the table.

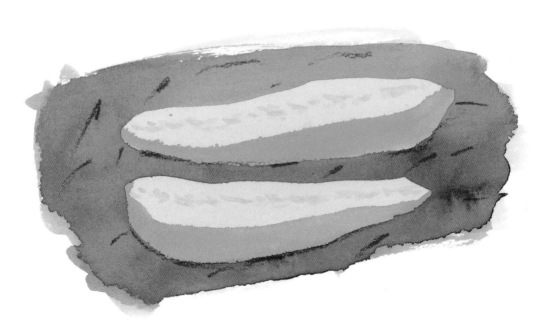

Gnocchi con salsa di pomodoro crudo e mozzarella
Gnocchi with Uncooked Fresh Tomato Sauce and Mozzarella
for 4–6 people

This recipe's light, refreshing summer sauce is delightful over steaming, freshly cooked pasta. It is a sauce of utmost simplicity, but it can succeed only if fresh, ripe, sweet tomatoes and extra virgin olive oil are used.

......

2 pounds sweet, fresh vine-ripened
   plum tomatoes or cherry tomatoes
½ cup extra virgin olive oil
¼ cup fresh basil leaves, torn into
   small pieces
½ pound fresh mozzarella, cut into
   small pieces
1¼ teaspoons salt, or to taste
¼ teaspoon red pepper flakes, or to
   taste
1½ tablespoons salt, for cooking
   pasta
1 pound gnocchi *(large dumplings),*
   medium-sized conchiglie
   ("shells"), spaghetti, or linguine

Blanch tomatoes for 30 seconds to facilitate peeling them. Remove skin, seeds, and any tough core near stem. Chop roughly. Combine with oil, basil, cheese, and salt and red pepper to taste. Flavor of sauce is improved if it is refrigerated for 1 to 2 hours. To cook the pasta, bring 4 to 5 quarts water to a boil and add the 1½ tablespoons salt and pasta. Stir, continuing to stir frequently to prevent pasta from sticking together. Taste pasta after 8 minutes; it should be cooked thoroughly but still be firm to the bite (al dente). If necessary, continue cooking. If in doubt, drain immediately—pasta will continue to cook while it is hot. Take care not to overdrain; pasta should be piping hot and still dripping a little when it is transferred to a serving bowl. Combine hot pasta with cold sauce. Serve immediately.

Variation: Substitute ¼ cup Nicoise or Kalamata olives sliced off the pit, and 1 tablespoon capers for the mozzarella.

Note: This sauce can be made and refrigerated several days in advance of use.

Linguine con aragosta all'Amendolara

Anna Amendolara's Linguine with Lobster Sauce

for 6 people

The recipe for this delicious dish is from Anna Amendolara Nurse, a gifted cook, talented cooking teacher, and friend. Despite the elegance of the dish, it is very easy to make. I almost always serve it for the traditional Italian Christmas Eve fish dinner, for which, because of the sheer number of fish dishes (seven) required, things must be kept simple.

3 or 4 live lobsters (1¼ to 1½ pounds each)
¾ cup olive oil
4 large cloves garlic, peeled and left whole
2 cans (28 ounces each) peeled tomatoes in purée
1 teaspoon dried oregano
½ cup chopped fresh Italian parsley leaves
salt to taste
2 small dried hot red peppers (optional)
2 tablespoons salt, for cooking pasta
1½ pounds linguine (dried, not fresh pasta)

Rinse live lobsters in cold water. Split them in half and then in quarters. Set aside. In a pan large enough to hold lobsters, combine olive oil and garlic, and cook over gentle heat until garlic is golden but not brown. Add lobsters and stir often until they turn red. Add tomatoes, oregano, parsley, salt to taste, and hot peppers, if used. Simmer gently, partially covered, until sauce has thickened slightly, about 30 minutes. To cook the pasta, bring 6 quarts water to a rapid boil. Add the 2 tablespoons salt and linguine and stir immediately, continuing to stir frequently as pasta cooks to prevent strands from sticking together. Cook until pasta is al dente, then drain and turn into a large heated bowl. Toss with lobster sauce. Serve lobster alongside of pasta or as a second course.

Linguine al pesto

Linguine with Basil Sauce
for 4 people

Uncooked basil sauce, now familiar to many Americans as pesto, originated in Genoa, in the Liguria region. It is one of the oldest Italian dishes known, said to have come about from the combined influence of the Arabs, Persians, and Byzantines. The Italians insist that it should be served with *trenette,* a narrow but thick homemade egg noodle, because the unctuous character of the sauce is too overwhelming for more delicate egg noodles. But pesto also works well with linguine, spaghetti, or even the larger *bucatini*. Saucing tortellini or other stuffed pasta with pesto creates too many conflicts with the flavors and textures of their fillings.

Authentic pesto can be made only with fresh basil leaves, but there are many variations of it. It can be made with pine nuts or walnuts, with or without butter, and with the addition of a small amount of parsley to quiet its natural sweetness. Some Italians add both parmigiano and *pecorino* cheeses, whereas other Italians, the Romans in particular, are horrified at the mere suggestion of introducing *pecorino* to pesto. *Pecorino* cheese is sharper and more salty than parmigiano. It would be a mistake to use it alone. A blend is suggested for this dish. If you will not be using the pesto immediately, leave out the cheeses, salt, and butter. Beat them in just before using the pesto.

⸬

3 cloves garlic, cut into pieces

2 cups solidly packed fresh basil
    leaves

generous ½ teaspoon salt

a twist or two of freshly milled black
    pepper

½ cup virgin olive oil

⅓ cup very lightly toasted pine nuts

½ cup freshly grated parmigiano

scant ¼ cup freshly grated Romano
    or pecorino cheese

2 tablespoons sweet (unsalted) but-
    ter, softened to room temperature

1½ tablespoons salt, for cooking
    pasta

1 pound linguine or spaghetti

Combine garlic, basil, the ½ teaspoon salt, pepper, oil, and pine nuts in a food processor and blend to a smooth purée, stopping machine once or twice to scrape sides of container with a rubber spatula so that all ingredients are equally ground. Add grated cheeses and butter, and process for about 15 seconds. Scrape sides again and process for another few seconds. Do not overgrind, or pesto will have very little texture. Bring 4 to 5 quarts water to a rapid boil and add the 1½ tablespoons salt and pasta. Stir immediately, and continue to stir frequently to prevent strands from sticking together. Drain, reserving some of the water. Do not overdrain; pasta should still be quite moist and dripping a little in order to combine properly with pesto. Stir 1 tablespoon of the hot water from drained pasta into pesto. Transfer pasta to a warm bowl, then toss with pesto. Serve immediately.

Note: For a pesto that is almost as quick, and with an even better texture, beat in the grated cheeses and butter by hand after you have finished blending the other ingredients in the food processor.

Keeping and freezing pesto: Pesto base will keep in the refrigerator for several months in a sealed glass jar. I have found the best way of preventing a dark layer from forming on the top is to press a layer of plastic wrap onto the surface of the pesto base. This is far more effective than the traditional method of pouring olive oil on the surface. You can freeze the pesto base in the same way.

Linguine alle vongole (versione bianca)
Linguine with White Clam Sauce
for 4 people

:::::

4 dozen littleneck clams

$1/3$ cup olive oil

5 cloves garlic, finely chopped

6 tablespoons chopped fresh Italian
  parsley leaves

$1/3$ cup dry white wine

$1/4$ teaspoon salt, or to taste

freshly milled black pepper

5 tablespoons fresh fine white bread
  crumbs, lightly toasted

$1^1/2$ tablespoons salt, for cooking
  pasta

1 pound thin linguine or spaghetti

If possible, several hours before cooking clams, place them in a bowl with cold water and a handful of flour or cornmeal so that they can purge themselves. Refrigerate. Scrub clams well when ready to use them. In a pan that will be large enough to hold clams, combine oil, 4 of the chopped garlic cloves, and 4 tablespoons of the chopped parsley. Sauté over gentle heat until garlic is softened but not colored, then add wine, the $1/4$ teaspoon salt, and pepper. Allow wine to evaporate for 3 minutes. Add scrubbed clams and steam over medium heat until clams open. Remove clams from half of the shells; return clams to sauce and discard shells. Remaining clams should be left intact to add color and character to sauce. Add bread crumbs and remaining garlic and parsley to sauce and toss well. Meanwhile, bring 4 to 5 quarts water to a rapid boil. Add the $1^1/2$ tablespoons salt and pasta. Stir immediately, and continue to stir frequently until pasta is al dente. Drain and combine with sauce in a large, warm bowl. Serve immediately. Do not serve with grated cheese (grated cheese should never be added to seafood sauces).

Maccheroncini alla puttanesca (versione cruda)

Harlot-Style Macaroni (Uncooked, Summer Version)

for 4 people

There are many versions in Italy of this spicy-sounding dish (see *Spaghetti alla puttanesca* for the cooked version). It could be that the name bestowed on the sauce arises from the quickness with which a nourishing meal had to be prepared between customers in Naples' legendary houses of ill repute. Or, the title might refer to the zesty ingredients that go into the sauce. In any case, this version, which is completely uncooked, and in which sweet, ripe summer tomatoes are essential, is quite different from the cooked version. It is preferable to refrigerate the sauce anywhere from 2 to 48 hours, but in a pinch I often make this dish to serve immediately, and find this spontaneous version delightful, as long as the tomatoes are ripe and sweet.

......

2½ pounds fresh, ripe, sweet tomatoes, peeled, seeded, and chopped

½ cup extra virgin olive oil

3 large cloves garlic, coarsely chopped

¼ cup sharp-flavored black olives (such as Gaeta, Nicoise, or Kalamata) sliced off the pit

1 tablespoon capers

chopped fresh hot pepper or dried hot pepper to taste

salt to taste

handful fresh basil leaves (about 10), torn into small pieces

1½ tablespoons salt, for cooking pasta

1 pound medium-sized macaroni, such as pennette *("little quills") or* fusilli *("twists")*

Blanch tomatoes for 30 seconds to facilitate peeling them. Remove skin, seeds, and any tough core near stem. Chop coarsely. In the bowl in which pasta will be served, combine oil, garlic, olives, capers, hot pepper and salt to taste, and basil. Set aside. Bring 4 to 5 quarts water to a rapid boil and add the 1½ tablespoons salt and pasta. Stir immediately, continuing to stir frequently to prevent strands from sticking together. Cook until pasta is al dente, then drain, and toss hot pasta with cool sauce. Serve immediately.

Maccheroni con sugo di broccoli

Macaroni with Broccoli Sauce

for 4 people

This dish is a specialty of Apulia, a part of southern Italy from which many immigrants came—my own paternal grandparents included. The dish never ceases to evoke in me a renewed love for real southern Italian food of the sort most Americans rarely experience. Don't be put off by the anchovies in the sauce—they dissolve completely into the hot olive oil and become part of the sauce. Even avowed anchovy haters for whom I have made this dish have loved it.

......

1 large head broccoli
1½ tablespoons salt
1 pound ziti, penne, penne rigate, or
  rigatoni
½ cup olive oil
1½ cans anchovy fillets in olive oil

Wash and trim broccoli, cutting off any tough or discolored parts. Divide top into florets, and slice stalk into approximately 2-inch-long, finger-sized pieces. Bring 7 quarts water to a rapid boil and add salt, broccoli, and pasta all at once. Cook until pasta is al dente, stirring several times to prevent pasta from sticking together and allow even cooking. Meanwhile, over gentle heat cook oil and anchovies together, including oil from 1 anchovy can. Anchovies will dissolve completely in oil, forming sauce. Drain pasta without overdraining—it should still be moist and dripping a little—and transfer to a warm bowl. Toss pasta and broccoli with anchovy sauce. Serve immediately. Don't serve with grated cheese (grated cheese should never be added to seafood sauces).

Mafalde al forno con melanzane, salsicce, e pecorino

Baked Fluted Noodles with Eggplant, Sausage, and *Pecorino* Cheese

for 6 people

The long, curly form and toothy texture of *mafalde* make this pasta well suited to the earthy ingredients in this rustic *pasticcio*.

⁓

1½ tablespoons salt, for cooking pasta

8 ounces mafalde *(long, wide, fluted dried pasta)*

1 can (28 ounces) plum tomatoes in purée

5 or 6 large fresh basil leaves, torn, or 1 teaspoon dried basil

3 tablespoons virgin or extra virgin olive oil

salt and freshly ground black pepper to taste

1½ pounds eggplant (2 medium eggplants)

1 pound lean, sweet, fennel-flavored Italian pork sausages (about 6 links), partially frozen

1 cup vegetable oil, for frying

1½ cups freshly grated parmigiano

½ pound Sardinian semi-soft pecorino *cheese or Tuscan* caciotta, *thinly sliced*

Preheat the oven to 350°. Add the 1½ tablespoons salt and pasta to 5 quarts rapidly boiling water. Stir immediately and continue to stir frequently while pasta cooks to prevent noodles from sticking together. Drain when slightly underdone, and rinse with cold water to prevent pasta from sticking together as it cools. Set aside. Place tomatoes and basil in a saucepan. Bring to a boil and immediately reduce heat to medium-low. Simmer for 30 minutes, uncovered, stirring occasionally. Sauce should be thick, not watery. If tomatoes seem excessively watery as they cook, drain off some of the liquid and resume simmering. If necessary, cook longer to thicken. Pass tomato mixture through a food mill to remove all seeds (puréeing in a food processor will not remove seeds). Add olive oil and salt and pepper to taste and set aside. Peel eggplants and discard stems. Cut into ¼-inch slices and sprinkle each on both sides with salt to release bitter liquor from seeds. Place slices vertically in a colander in the sink for 30 minutes to allow liquor to drain off. Pat eggplant well with paper towels to remove excess salt and remaining liquor from seeds. Slip casings off sausages and slice them thin (possible only if sausages are partially frozen). Heat 2 tablespoons of the vegetable oil in a large skillet over medium heat, and brown sausage slices on both sides. Drain on paper towels and set aside. Heat remaining vegetable oil in skillet. When oil is hot enough for eggplant to sizzle in it, fry slices until golden brown on both sides. Drain on paper towels. Smear several tablespoons of reserved sauce in a 10- by 12-inch baking dish that is 3 inches deep, and cover with a third of the pasta. Moisten with more sauce. Top with half the eggplant and cover with a thin layer of sauce. Add half the sausage, and sprinkle with grated parmigiano and sliced *pecorino*. Repeat layering, ending with pasta smeared with sauce and sprinkled with both cheeses. Cover with foil and bake in preheated oven for 20 minutes. Remove foil and bake until heated through and bubbly, about 10 minutes more. Allow to settle for 10 minutes. Serve.

Note: This dish can be made several days in advance of cooking; it freezes well.

Pappardelle coi funghi selvatici

Pappardelle with Wild Mushrooms

for 4 people

Pappardelle are the widest Italian egg noddles, the perfect shape to combine with the thinly sliced, fan-shaped caps of the wild mushrooms in this sauce. The noodles can be made at home, or bought in dried form from an Italian grocer. The more widely available fettucine or *tagliatelle* can, however, be substituted.

......

6 ounces fresh wild mushrooms,
  such as shiitake or chanterelle,
  or a combination
½ cup extra-virgin olive oil
6 large cloves garlic, chopped
6 tablespoons chopped fresh
  Italian parsley leaves
⅔ cup chicken stock
salt and freshly milled black pepper
  to taste
1½ tablespoons salt, for cooking pasta
1 pound fresh or dried pappardelle,
  fettucine, or tagliatelle
freshly grated parmigiano,
  for the table (optional)

Brush any soil off mushrooms with a soft brush or clean kitchen towel. Do not wash them. Trim bottoms off stems if they are tough, and slice mushrooms lengthwise. In a large skillet over medium heat, combine oil, garlic, and parsley, and cook until garlic is softened. Add mushrooms and sauté for 2 to 3 minutes. Add chicken stock and continue to sauté until mushrooms are tender, 4 to 5 minutes. Add salt and pepper to taste. Meanwhile, bring 4 to 5 quarts water to a rapid boil. Add the 1½ tablespoons salt and pasta and stir immediately, continuing to stir frequently to prevent pasta ribbons from sticking together. Drain but don't overdrain—pasta should be dripping somewhat when combined with sauce. Transfer pasta to skillet with sauce. Toss well and serve. Pass parmigiano at the table, if using.

Pasta coi bisi alla Veneziana

Pasta and Peas Venetian Style

for 4 or 5 people

Peas, dried or fresh, are often used in Italian soups. There is no equal to freshly picked peas, but lacking access to the garden-fresh variety, use frozen peas. This light soup is to be served for lunch or dinner.

....

2 ounces pancetta *or lean bacon, very finely chopped*

2 tablespoons sweet (unsalted) butter

1 small onion, very finely chopped

1 package (10 ounces) frozen sweet baby peas, or 2 cups fresh shelled sweet baby peas, if available

3 tablespoons chopped fresh Italian parsley leaves

6 cups homemade or good-quality chicken broth

2 ounces fresh pappardelle *or dried egg noodles*

2 teaspoons salt

generous pinch of freshly milled white or black pepper

freshly grated parmigiano, for the table

If using bacon, blanch it for 30 seconds and allow to cool. Chop very fine. Sauté *pancetta* and butter in a saucepan over medium heat until *pancetta* begins to color. Add onion and sauté until softened. Add peas and cook gently for several minutes so flavors meld. Add parsley and 1 cup of the stock. Simmer very gently for 5 minutes. Add remaining stock and bring it to a boil. Add pasta and immediately reduce to a gentle simmer. Cook until pasta is tender but not mushy, 5 to 7 minutes more. Add salt and pepper and serve. Pass parmigiano at the table.

Pasta e fagioli alla Toscana

Pasta and Bean Soup Tuscan Style

for 4 people

......

¼ pound dry cannellini beans

4 tablespoons extra virgin olive oil,
   plus more for the table

2 large cloves garlic, bruised

1 pound very ripe vine-ripened
   tomatoes, peeled, seeded, and
   chopped, or 1 cup canned plum
   tomatoes, drained, seeded, and
   chopped

1½ teaspoons fresh rosemary or ¾
   teaspoon dried rosemary

4 cups cold water

1 cup ditalini ("little thimbles")

2 teaspoons salt, or to taste

freshly milled black pepper to taste

Soak beans overnight. The following day, pick over and rinse well in cold water. In a large stockpot over gentle heat, combine the 4 tablespoons oil and garlic, and cook until garlic is golden but not brown. Add tomatoes and rosemary and cook gently for 5 minutes. Add rinsed beans and the water. Bring to a boil, then reduce to a simmer and cook gently until beans are tender, about 1 hour. Scoop out half of the beans and mash or purée them. Return purée to pot. Add pasta and salt and continue to cook gently until it is al dente. Allow soup to rest for 1 hour so flavors meld, or serve lukewarm the next day. The soup will be quite dense—more like a stew. Serve with plenty of freshly milled black pepper and virgin olive oil drizzled over each portion at the table.

Pasticcio di lasagne col ragù
Lasagne Casserole with Meat and Red Wine Sauce
for 6 people as a main course

Americans think of lasagna as the name for a layered pasta casserole. Actually, the word *lasagna* means a wide, flat, long noodle; lasagne is the plural. In the north of Italy, lasagne are usually made from fresh, homemade egg or spinach pasta rolled into the thinnest possible strips of dough, because so many layers (between 10 and 12) are placed one on top of the other with layers of sauce or sauces and cheese in between. In the south of Italy, a *pasticcio*—casserole—of lasagne is most often prepared with semolina pasta, either homemade or hard, factory made. Southern Italian sauces are more rustic than the refined, creamy meat sauces typical of the north. In the South, soft cheeses, such as mozzarella and ricotta, are placed between the layers of pasta, whereas in northern Italian cooking, béchamel and grated parmigiano are used. No effort is spared when this dish is being prepared for *carnevale,* carnival festivities. It typically includes cooked sliced ham, tiny veal meatballs, and more sausages between the layers of pasta. Because what is commercially sold as "fresh" pasta in this country is not thin enough for a proper lasagne dish that contains many layers of pasta, and also because I find the flavor and texture of this imposter objectionable, I do not recommend using it. To make a classic lasagne with delicate, homemade pasta, see the chapter on Festive and Baked Specialties in my book *Pasta Classica: The Art of Italian Pasta Cooking* (Chronicle Books, 1987). For a quicker, more rustic lasagne dish, I offer this recipe of southern origin using hard, factory-made semolina noodles. The flavor of this dish is improved by preparing it in advance, or allowing it to cool and reheating it.

Sauce

½ ounce dried porcini *mushrooms*

3 tablespoons olive oil

3 tablespoons sweet (unsalted) butter

1 medium to large onion, finely chopped

1 large clove garlic, finely chopped

3 tablespoons chopped fresh Italian parsley leaves

1 large carrot, scraped and finely chopped

1 large stalk celery, including leaves, finely chopped

½ pound lean, sweet, fennel-flavored Italian pork sausages (about 3 links)

1 pound lean ground beef or pork

4 tablespoons tomato paste

¾ cup good dry red wine

1 can (28 ounces) tomatoes in purée, drained and coarsely chopped, purée reserved

1½ teaspoons salt, or to taste

freshly milled black pepper to taste

2 tablespoons salt, for cooking pasta

2 tablespoons vegetable oil

1 pound dried lasagne or narrower lasagnette noodles

1½ pounds (3 cups) ricotta cheese

good pinch of freshly grated nutmeg

1½ cups freshly grated parmigiano

½ pound thinly sliced Italian sala-me, *such as* soppressata, *diced*

1½ pounds good-quality mozzarella, cut into very thin slices, or shredded

Soak dried mushrooms in ¼ cup warm water until softened, about 30 minutes. Strain liquid through a fine sieve; reserve. Chop mushrooms coarsely. Set aside. Heat olive oil and butter in a heavy saucepan. Add onion, garlic, parsley, carrot, and celery; sauté over medium heat until vegetables are softened, about 10 minutes; do not let them brown. Remove sausage meat from casings. Add it and ground meat to pan; sauté until lightly browned, about 8 minutes, breaking up meat with a spoon and mixing it with vegetables. Sauté gently another 8 to 10 minutes. Stir in reserved mushrooms and their liquor, tomato paste, and wine; simmer 5 minutes. Add tomatoes and their reserved purée; simmer gently, uncovered, until sauce thickens, about 30 minutes. Season with salt and pepper. Meanwhile, preheat the oven to 425°. Bring 5 to 6 quarts water to a rolling boil and add the 2 tablespoons salt, vegetable oil, and noodles. Stir immediately, continuing to stir frequently as noodles cook. Drain when slightly underdone (they will continue to cook in the oven), reserving ⅓ cup of the cooking water. Immediately rinse lasagne well in cold water to prevent noodles from sticking together.

Combine ricotta with reserved pasta water, nutmeg, and ½ cup of the parmigiano. Smear the bottom of a 10- by 14-inch baking pan with a little of the meat sauce. Then place a single solid layer of noodles on top, without overlapping. Spread a layer of ricotta mixture on noodles, followed by a layer of sauce. Sprinkle with some of the *salame*, add a layer of mozzarella, then sprinkle with several teaspoons of the remaining parmigiano. Repeat layering until all ingredients are used up, ending with a layer of meat sauce strewn with mozzarella and parmigiano. Be sure to cover pasta with sauce to prevent it from drying out in the oven. Slide pan onto rack in upper half of preheated oven. Bake until lasagne is heated through and bubbly, about 25 minutes. Remove from oven and let settle for 10 to 15 minutes. Cut into squares and serve as a main course.

Pasticcio di pennette ai frutti di mare e asparagi
Casserole of "Little Quills," Seafood, and Asparagus
for 6 people as a main course

This dish is substantial and delicate at the same time. It is a great party dish because of its elegant ingredients and color.

......

1½ tablespoons salt, for cooking pasta

1 pound pennette *or other short macaroni, such as* penne, penne rigate, *short* ziti, *or medium-sized shells*

Béchamel Sauce

3 tablespoons sweet (unsalted) butter

2 tablespoons plus 1 teaspoon flour

2½ cups hot milk

½ teaspoon salt, or to taste

freshly milled white pepper to taste

6 ounces fresh asparagus (6 to 8 spears)

½ pound fresh shrimp, shelled and deveined

½ pound bay or sea scallops

4 tablespoons sweet (unsalted) butter

¼ pound precooked lump crabmeat, flaked

¾ cup good dry white wine

¼ teaspoon salt, or to taste

½ teaspoon dried green peppercorns, pulverized with a mortar and pestle, or freshly milled black pepper to taste

Preheat the oven to 375°. Add the 1½ tablespoons salt and pasta to 5 quarts rapidly boiling water. Stir immediately, and continue to stir frequently while pasta cooks to prevent it from sticking together. Drain when slightly underdone. Rinse with cold water to prevent pasta from sticking together as it cools. Meanwhile, prepare béchamel. Melt butter and stir in flour with a wooden spoon. When flour has been absorbed, add hot milk little by little, stirring continuously. It is critical to add milk gradually, or mixture will form lumps. Continue stirring constantly after all milk has been added until sauce is thick enough to lightly coat spoon—it should not be too thick. Season with salt and pepper. Place a piece of plastic wrap directly on surface of sauce to prevent a skin from forming, and set aside. Trim any tough parts off asparagus and poach or steam until nearly tender but not too soft. Set aside. Cut shrimp in half lengthwise. If using sea scallops, slice them in half crosswise—or into thirds if the scallops are very large—to make thin medallions. In a large skillet over medium heat, melt butter; add shrimp and sauté until pink on both sides but not cooked through, 1 to 2 minutes. Add scallops and cook lightly on both sides. Add crabmeat, wine, salt, and peppercorns; toss. Simmer gently for 3 minutes to allow alcohol to evaporate. Remove wrap from béchamel and place sauce over gentle heat. Using a wooden spoon, stir all liquid from seafood into béchamel, thoroughly mixing liquids. Taste and adjust seasonings if necessary. Smear a little sauce on the bottom of a 10- by 12-inch baking dish that is 3 inches deep. Combine pasta, sauce, and seafood, tossing well to distribute ingredients. Transfer to baking dish. Place reserved asparagus on top of pasticcio. Cover tightly with foil and bake until heated through, 20 to 25 minutes. Allow to settle for 5 to 10 minutes. Serve. Don't serve with grated cheese (grated cheese should never be added to seafood sauces).

Note: This dish can be made up to a day in advance of baking or frozen until you are ready to bake.

Pasticcio di tagliatelle, fegatini, funghi, e prosciutto

Casserole of Egg Noodles, Chicken Livers, Wild Mushrooms, and Ham

for 4–6 people as a main course

This dish is a classic harmony of Italian flavors. It is intensely flavored yet wonderfully delicate because of the use of egg noodles, cream, and butter.

....

5 tablespoons sweet (unsalted) butter, plus enough for greasing baking dish

1½ tablespoons salt, for cooking pasta

8 ounces dried tagliatelle *or egg noodles*

½ pound fresh shiitake, chanterelle, or other wild mushrooms

4 ounces plump fresh chicken livers, cleaned and quartered

3 or 4 chopped fresh sage leaves, or ¼ teaspoon crumbled dried sage

1 medium onion, chopped

4 ounces ham, cut into strips

½ cup good dry white wine

2 eggs, lightly beaten

⅔ cup heavy cream

½ cup freshly grated parmigiano

½ teaspoon salt

freshly milled black pepper to taste

1 teaspoon chopped fresh Italian parsley leaves

2 tablespoons fine white bread crumbs

Preheat the oven to 375°. Have ready a buttered baking dish, approximately 10 by 12 inches and 2 to 3 inches deep. Add the 1½ tablespoons salt and pasta to 5 quarts rapidly boiling water. Stir immediately and frequently while pasta cooks to prevent noodles from sticking together. Drain when slightly underdone. Rinse with cold water to prevent noodles from sticking to each other as they cool. Meanwhile, remove soil from mushrooms with a soft brush or clean dish towel. Cut off and discard any woody stems. Slice mushrooms thinly. Melt 1 tablespoon of the butter in a small skillet over medium-high heat and sauté chicken livers until they are browned but still slightly pink inside. Set aside. In a larger skillet, melt 3 tablespoons of the butter; add sage and onion and cook over gentle heat until onion is soft but not brown. Add ham and mushrooms and sauté until mushrooms are tender, tossing to cook evenly and distribute butter. Add wine and cook for another 3 minutes to evaporate alcohol. In a large bowl mix eggs, cream, parmigiano, the ½ teaspoon salt, pepper, and parsley. Add ham and mushroom mixture and reserved chicken livers. Add pasta and toss well. Transfer to buttered baking dish. Heat remaining tablespoon butter with bread crumbs until all butter is absorbed and mixture is crumbly. Sprinkle it over *pasticcio*. Cover with foil and bake for 25 minutes. Allow to settle for 5 to 10 minutes, and serve.

Note: This *pasticcio* can be baked in advance and reheated. To reheat in the microwave, cover with plastic wrap and use highest setting (length of time will depend on microwave). To reheat in the oven, moisten pasta with a little stock or light cream to prevent it from drying out. Cover tightly with foil and bake on upper rack of preheated 400° oven until heated through, about 20 minutes.

Penne alle melanzane

"Quills" with Eggplant Sauce

for 4–6 people

The sauce for this pasta dish can be made well in advance of serving, even up to four to five days ahead. Select eggplants that are ripe but not excessively large and seedy; their skins should be smooth, not wrinkled, indicating freshness.

......

1¼ to 1½ pounds eggplant (2 medium eggplants)
salt, for sprinkling on eggplant
2 large cloves garlic, finely chopped
1 medium onion, finely chopped
½ cup chopped fresh Italian parsley leaves
½ teaspoon dried green peppercorns, crushed with a mortar and pestle, or freshly milled black pepper to taste
¼ cup virgin olive oil
1½ tablespoons salt, for cooking pasta
1 pound penne, ziti, bucatini, *or* perciatelli *(small pierced macaroni)*

2 tablespoons sweet (unsalted) butter

Preheat the oven to 400°. Cut eggplants lengthwise into ¼-inch slices. Sprinkle both sides of each slice with salt to release bitter liquor from seeds. Stand slices in a colander in the sink so liquor that is released runs off. Allow to drain for 30 to 40 minutes. Meanwhile, in a large skillet over medium-low heat, combine garlic, onion, parsley, pepper, and 3 tablespoons of the oil, and sauté until onion and garlic are softened but not brown. Wipe salt off eggplant slices with a clean paper towel. If there are excessive seeds, scrape out some of them. Brush eggplant slices on both sides with remaining oil and place on a baking sheet. Bake in preheated oven until tender, about 30 minutes. When cool enough to handle, remove and discard peel from eggplant slices. Chop eggplant finely and combine well with sautéed garlic mixture. Taste and adjust seasonings if necessary. To cook the pasta, bring 4 to 5 quarts water to a boil and add 1½ tablespoons salt and pasta. Stir, continuing to stir frequently to prevent pasta from sticking together. Taste pasta after 8 minutes; it should be cooked thoroughly but still be firm to the bite (al dente). If necessary, continue cook-

ing. If in doubt, drain immediately (reserve some cooking water)—pasta will continue to cook while it is hot. Take care not to over-drain; pasta should be piping hot and still dripping when it is transferred to a serving bowl. Have a large, heated bowl waiting with butter in it. Add 2 tablespoons pasta cooking water to sauce to help make sauce creamy. Combine pasta and sauce. Serve immediately.

Penne con polpa di granchio

"Quills" with Crabmeat

for 4–6 people

This is a simply lovely way of combining seafood with pasta. The crabmeat remains chunky, so it is best to select a type of macaroni that will cradle the seafood, thus capturing a little bit of crab with each forkful.

....

1 can (28 ounces) peeled plum to-
matoes in their own juice
4 tablespoons virgin olive oil
1 medium onion, finely chopped
3 tablespoons chopped fresh Italian
parsley leaves
¼ cup dry white wine
½ pound precooked lump crabmeat,
flaked
salt and freshly milled white pepper
to taste
1½ tablespoons salt, for cooking
pasta
1 pound penne, pennette, creste di
gallo *("cockscombs"), or* riccini
("curls")

Separate tomatoes from their juice. Remove excess seeds in tomatoes but do not rinse them (flavor will be lost with rinsing). Chop tomatoes. Strain juice to remove seeds. Set both aside. In a large skillet or saucepan over gentle heat, combine oil, onion, and parsley, and cook until onion is completely soft but not brown. Add strained tomato juice and simmer over medium heat to reduce, 10 minutes. Add chopped tomatoes and wine. Simmer gently until alcohol evaporates, about 5 minutes. Add crabmeat and salt and pepper to taste. (Seasoning will depend on flavor of crabmeat to some extent.) Simmer gently an additional 5 minutes, taking care not to overcook delicate crabmeat. To cook the pasta, bring 4 to 5 quarts water to a boil and add the 1½ tablespoons salt and pasta. Stir, continuing to stir frequently to prevent pasta from sticking together. Taste pasta after 8 minutes; it should be cooked thoroughly but still be firm to the bite (al dente). If necessary, continue cooking. If in doubt, drain immediately—pasta will continue to cook while it is hot. Take care not to overdrain; pasta should be piping hot and still dripping when it is transferred to a serving bowl. In a large, heated bowl, combine pasta and sauce. Serve immediately. Don't serve with grated cheese (grated cheese should never be added to seafood sauces).

Spaghetti alla carbonara di magro

Spaghetti with Bacon and Egg Sauce (Lean Version)

for 4–6 people

I have heard several theories about the origins of this dish, but whatever its true history, *carbonara* (from *carbone*, or coal) presumably refers to the generous sprinkling of coal-like black pepper over the dish. The Italians make this dish with *pancetta*, a subtly spiced, not smoked, variety of bacon. Canadian ham or lean bacon substitutes nicely.

2 tablespoons extra-virgin olive oil
2 large cloves garlic, bruised
⅓ pound diced pancetta, *ham,*
* or lean bacon*
5 eggs
¾ cup freshly grated parmigiano
salt to taste
plenty of freshly ground black pepper
1½ tablespoons salt, for cooking pasta
1 pound spaghetti

In a large skillet over medium-low heat, combine oil and garlic, and cook until garlic is golden; do not allow it to brown, or it will impart a bitter flavor to the sauce. Add *pancetta*, ham, or bacon to skillet and sauté until golden. If excessively fatty, drain off all but 2 tablespoons of the pan drippings and set aside. Meanwhile, in a medium bowl, beat eggs, cheese, and salt and pepper to taste, and set aside. Bring 4 to 5 quarts of water to a rapid boil. Add the 1½ tablespoons salt and pasta and stir immediately, continuing to stir frequently to prevent pasta ribbons from sticking together. When spaghetti is al dente, drain it, taking care not to overdrain; it should still be dripping when transferred to a serving bowl, or pasta will be too dry.

Immediately add reserved egg mixture—pasta must be at its hottest in order for eggs to "cook." Add ham or bacon and the 2 tablespoons drippings; toss together. Serve immediately—this dish must be eaten piping hot.

Spaghetti alla puttanesca

Spaghetti with Harlot's Sauce (Cooked Version)

for 4–6 people

This racy, earthy dish is a specialty of raucous, colorful Naples. There are (perhaps aptly) hot and cold versions of *spaghetti alla puttanesca*. Here is the hot; see *Maccheroncini alla puttanesca (versione cruda)* for the cold version.

1 can (28 ounces) plum tomatoes in
  their own juice, or crushed plum
  tomatoes
3 tablespoons virgin olive oil
3 large cloves garlic, cut into pieces
1 small red or yellow bell pepper,
  cored, seeded, and diced
3 tablespoons chopped fresh Italian
  parsley leaves
½ teaspoon dried oregano or 1 teaspoon fresh oregano
3 anchovy fillets (the variety packed
  in olive oil), cut up
3 tablespoons sharp-flavored black
  olives (such as Gaeta, Nicoise, or
  Kalamata) sliced off the pit
½ teaspoon red pepper flakes
1 tablespoon capers
salt to taste, plus 1½ tablespoons
  salt, for cooking pasta
1 pound spaghetti

Separate tomatoes from their juice. Remove excess seeds from tomatoes but do not rinse them (flavor will be lost with rinsing). Chop tomatoes. Strain juice to remove seeds. Set both aside. In a large skillet over medium heat, combine oil, garlic, bell pepper, parsley, and oregano, and sauté until vegetables are soft. Add anchovies and stir. Add chopped tomatoes and strained juice, olives, red pepper flakes, and capers. Simmer for 20 minutes. Add salt to taste. To cook the pasta, bring 4 to 5 quarts water to a rolling boil and add the 1½ tablespoons salt and pasta. Stir, and continue to stir frequently to prevent pasta from sticking together. Taste pasta after 8 minutes; it should be cooked thoroughly but still be firm to the bite (al dente). If necessary, continue cooking. If in doubt, drain immediately—pasta will continue to cook while it is hot. Take care not to overdrain; pasta should be piping hot and still dripping when it is transferred to a serving bowl. Have a large, heated bowl waiting with sauce in it. Combine pasta and sauce. Serve immediately. No grated cheese is required. It would interfere with the other strong flavors in the sauce.

Spaghetti alle vongole col pomodoro
Spaghetti with Clam Sauce and Fresh Tomato
for 4 people

Is there any dish more reminiscent than this of the proverbial Italian repast, eaten by moonlight at some romantic seaside spot—say, Amalfi or Sorrento? It was not until I took my first trip to southern Italy that I knew what this dish should really taste like, and perhaps it was the grip of love that made it so indescribably beguiling. But even in my New York kitchen, there is a certain magic in this dish, and I cook it regularly.

3 dozen littleneck clams

$^1/_3$ cup extra virgin olive oil

4 large cloves garlic, chopped

4 tablespoons chopped fresh Italian
  parsley leaves

3 large ripe tomatoes, peeled,
  seeded, and chopped

$^1/_2$ cup clam juice or dry white wine

salt and freshly milled black pepper
  to taste

$1^1/_2$ tablespoons salt, for cooking
  pasta

1 pound spaghetti or thin linguine

Italian or French bread, for the
  table

If possible, several hours before cooking clams, place them in a bowl with cold water and a handful of flour or cornmeal so that they can purge themselves. Refrigerate. Scrub clams well before using. In a large skillet over medium-low heat, combine oil, garlic, and parsley, and cook until garlic softens. Add tomatoes and allow to simmer 2 to 3 minutes. Add clam juice or wine and simmer gently 3 to 4 minutes. Add scrubbed clams, cover tightly, and steam over medium heat until clams open. Add salt and pepper to taste. Meanwhile, bring 4 to 5 quarts water to a rapid boil. Add the $1^1/_2$ table-spoons salt and pasta. Stir immediately and continue to stir frequently to prevent strands from sticking together. Cook until pasta is al dente. Drain and immediately add pasta to clam sauce in skillet; toss. Serve immediately. Do not add grated cheese (grated cheese should never be added to seafood sauces). Pass Italian or French bread at the table for soaking up clam sauce left in plates—not a drop should go to waste!

Spaghetti al tonno (versione bianca)
Spaghetti with Tuna Sauce (White Version)
for 4 people

The classic, practically effortless Italian sauce in this dish can be cooked in the time it takes the pasta to boil. Be sure to use Italian belly tuna packed in olive oil, which is tender, moist, very flavorful—and widely available in supermarkets. I would advise against substituting American-packed albacore tuna, especially tuna packed in water, which is bland and far too dry to create this sauce.

......

¼ cup extra virgin olive oil

2 large cloves garlic, chopped

2 anchovy fillets (the variety packed in olive oil), chopped

3 tablespoons chopped fresh Italian parsley leaves

1 can (6½ ounces) Italian tuna in olive oil, flaked, oil reserved

red pepper flakes to taste

½ cup chicken stock or dry white wine

1½ tablespoons salt, for cooking pasta

1 pound spaghetti

In a large skillet over gentle heat, combine oil, garlic, anchovies, and parsley, and cook until garlic is softened and anchovies are disintegrated. Add tuna and its oil, and red pepper to taste. With a fork break up tuna and flake it well. Add stock or wine and simmer for 5 minutes. Meanwhile, bring 4 to 5 quarts water to a rapid boil. Add salt and pasta and stir, continuing to stir frequently to prevent strands from sticking together. Cook until pasta is al dente, then drain (don't overdrain; it should still be somewhat dripping) and toss with sauce. Serve immediately. Don't serve with grated cheese (grated cheese should never be added to seafood sauces).

Spaghetti al tonno (versione rossa)

Spaghetti with Tuna Sauce (Red Version)

for 4–6 people

.....

¼ cup extra virgin or virgin olive oil

3 large cloves garlic, chopped

3 tablespoons chopped fresh Italian parsley leaves

1 teaspoon dried oregano or 2 teaspoons fresh oregano

1 can (28 ounces) crushed plum tomatoes or plum tomatoes in purée, seeded and chopped, liquid reserved

1 can (6½ ounces) Italian light-meat tuna in olive oil, flaked

1¼ teaspoons salt

½ teaspoon crushed dried green peppercorns, or freshly milled black pepper to taste

1½ tablespoons salt, for cooking pasta

1 pound spaghetti, linguine, or bucatini

In a large skillet over gentle heat, combine oil, garlic, and herbs, and cook until garlic softens—do not let it brown. Add tomatoes and their liquids, stir, and simmer for 10 minutes. Add tuna, the 1¼ teaspoons salt, and pepper, and simmer for another 5 minutes. Taste and adjust seasonings if necessary. Meanwhile, bring 4 to 5 quarts water to a rapid boil. Add the 1½ tablespoons salt and pasta and stir, continuing to stir frequently to prevent strands from sticking together. Taste pasta after 8 minutes; it should be cooked thoroughly but still be firm to the bite. If necessary, continue cooking. If in doubt, drain immediately—pasta will continue to cook while it is hot. Take care not to overdrain; pasta should be piping hot and still dripping when it is transferred to a serving bowl. Have a large, heated bowl waiting containing sauce. Toss pasta and sauce. Serve immediately. Don't serve with grated cheese (grated cheese should never be added to seafood sauces).

Spaghettini con le capesante
Thin Spaghetti with Scallops
for 3 people

The simple seafood sauce in this dish is well suited to dried pasta. While sea scallops are not as delicate in flavor as bay scallops, I have found their direct flavor an asset in this sauce.

½ pound sea scallops

4 tablespoons extra virgin olive oil

6 medium cloves garlic, grated

2 cups chopped canned plum tomatoes with ½ cup of their juices

1 heaping tablespoon tomato paste

⅓ cup dry vermouth

⅓ cup fresh basil leaves, chopped

½ teaspoon salt, or to taste

¼ teaspoon freshly ground white pepper

1½ tablespoons salt, for cooking pasta

12 ounces spaghettini *(thin spaghetti, but* not *"angel's hair")*

Wash and thoroughly dry scallops with a clean kitchen towel; slice each into three pieces. Set aside. In a large skillet over gentle heat, combine oil and garlic, and cook until garlic softens. Add chopped tomatoes without juices, and sauté gently for 4 to 5 minutes. Dissolve tomato paste in tomato juices; add to pan along with vermouth, and allow to evaporate over medium heat for about 4 minutes. Add basil, salt and pepper to taste, and scallops; sauté over medium heat for 3 minutes. Taste and adjust seasonings if necessary. Meanwhile, bring 4 to 5 quarts water to a rolling boil. Add the 1½ tablespoons salt and pasta and stir immediately. Cook, stirring frequently to prevent strands from sticking together, until pasta is al dente, about 7 minutes. Drain and toss with sauce. Serve immediately. Don't serve with grated cheese (grated cheese should never be added to seafood sauces).

Zuppa di cavolo e fagioli cannellini con tagliatelle
Cabbage and *Cannellini* Bean Soup with Pasta

for 4 people

....

4 ounces dry cannellini beans

8 cups water or chicken or veal stock

2 bay leaves

4 teaspoons salt

3 tablespoons sweet (unsalted) butter

1 medium onion, chopped

2 large cloves garlic, bruised

1 pound cabbage, quartered and cut into thin ribbons

2 ounces egg noodles

salt and plenty of freshly milled black pepper to taste

freshly grated parmigiano cheese, for the table

Soak beans overnight. Pick over and discard any small stones, and rinse beans well. Place beans in a pot with the water or stock and bay leaves. Bring to a boil; reduce to a simmer, partially cover, and cook until tender, 30 to 45 minutes. Add 2 teaspoons of the salt. Meanwhile, combine butter, onion, and garlic in a pot that will be large enough to hold beans and their liquid. Sauté gently until garlic is softened. Add cabbage and stir. Cover and cook over low heat until cabbage is soft, 15 to 20 minutes, stirring occasionally. Meanwhile, bring 5 to 6 cups water to a rolling boil. Add the remaining 2 teaspoons salt and pasta. Stir, continuing to stir frequently to prevent pasta from sticking together. Cook until pasta is tender but firm (al dente), then drain and add to cabbage and beans. Add salt and pepper to taste. Stir, and serve immediately. Pass parmigiano at the table.

Zuppa di lenticchie e ditalini con salsiccia

Lentil Soup with Sausages and "Little Thimbles"

for 6 people

A substantial soup pasta is needed in a hearty soup such as this, which contains lentils and large pieces of sausage. *Ditalini* ("little thimbles") are sturdy enough for the task but not so large as to overwhelm the small lentils. *Conchigliette* ("little shells") would also be a good choice.

·····

½ pound (1½ cups) brown lentils
10 cups chicken stock or water
1 tablespoon salt
1 bay leaf
5 links lean, sweet, fennel-flavored
  Italian pork sausages
2 tablespoons olive oil
3 medium cloves garlic, finely
  chopped
1 small onion, chopped
1 stalk celery, including leaves,
  finely chopped
2 teaspoons fresh thyme or 1 tea-
  spoon dried thyme

4 medium ripe tomatoes, or half a
  28-ounce can peeled plum toma-
  toes, seeded and chopped, liquid
  reserved
2 tablespoons tomato paste
½ cup ditalini or conchigliette
salt and freshly milled black pepper
  to taste
fresh Italian parsley leaves,
  chopped, for garnish

Pick over and wash lentils in cold water. Transfer to a large pot, cover with stock or water, and add the 1 tablespoon salt and bay leaf. Bring to a boil. Immediately reduce heat and cook gently for 10 minutes. Meanwhile, slip casings off sausages. Make a *soffritto* by heating oil in a large skillet and browning sausage meat in it. Add garlic and onion and sauté 2 minutes. Add celery, thyme, and chopped tomatoes and their liquid. Add tomato paste that has been dissolved in a little of the lentil broth. Stir. Add *soffritto* and pasta to lentils. Simmer 5 minutes. Add salt and pepper to taste. Cover and let rest until pasta is completely cooked, several more minutes. Sprinkle with parsley and serve.

Anellini ("little rings") Use in broths.

Bucatini (long, thin, hollow tubes) Use with pesto and with sauces containing *pancetta*, vegetables, cheeses.

Capelli d'angelo ("angel hair") Use in broths.

Capellini ("fine hair") Use in broths, with delicate seived tomato sauces and other light, smooth sauces, in *pasticci*.

Conchiglie ("shells") Use with tomato sauces, simple butter sauces, meat sauces.

Conchigliette ("little shells") Use in light soups.

Creste di Gallo ("cockscombs") Use with tomato sauces, meat sauces, creamy cheese sauces, combine with small beans.

Ditalini ("little thimbles") Use in soups with lentils or peas.

Farfalle ("butterflies") Use with simple oil-based sauces, butter sauces, tomato sauces, cheese sauces.

Fafalline ("little butterflies") Use in broths.

Fettucine ("little ribbons") Use with cream sauces.

Fusilli ("short twists") Use with *ragù*, meat sauces, ricotta sauces.

Gemelli ("twins") Use with meat, vegetable, and creamy cheese sauces.

Gnocchi (large "dumplings") Use with tomato sauces, butter sauces, meat sauces.

Linguine ("little tongues") Use with pesto, delicate oil-based sauces, white clam sauces.

Mafalde (long, wide, fluted noodle) Use with vegetable sauces, thick meat sauces, cream sauces, cheese sauces.

Orecchiette ("little ears") Use in thick soups, with sauces made from broccoli rabe, vegetable sauces, meat sauces, *ragù*.

Penne ("little quills") Use with tomato sauces, chunky tomato sauces, cream sauces.

Pennette ("little quills") Use with tomato sauces, meat sauces, cream sauces.

Perciatelli ("small pierced" macaroni) Use with *ragù*, meat sauces, baked *pasticci* with eggplant.

Radiatori ("wheels") Use with *ragù*, meat sauces, ricotta sauces.

Rigatoni ("large grooved" macaroni) Use with meat sauces, fresh tomato sauces, vegetable sauces, baked *timballi*.

Spaghetti ("a length of cord") Use with fillet of tomato sauce, oil-based sauces, pesto, fish sauces.

Spaghettini ("little length of cord") Use for *aglio e olio* (garlic and oil) sauce, delicate oil-based sauces, fish or clam sauces.

Stelline ("little stars") Use in broths.

Tagliatelle (from *tagliare*, "to cut") Use with cream sauces.

Ziti ("bridegrooms") Use with meat, vegetable sauces, baked *timballi*.